CODE BOOK

TOP SECRET

Dan Newman

MACMILLAN CHILDREN'S BOOKS

First published 2012 by Macmillan Children's Books
a division of Macmillan Publishers Limited
20 New Wharf Road, London N1 9RR
Basingstoke and Oxford
Associated companies throughout the world
www.panmacmillan.com

ISBN 978-1-4472-1632-2

1 3 5 7 9 8 6 4 2

A CIP catalogue record for this book is available from
the British Library.

Printed and bound by CPI Group (UK) Ltd, Croydon CR0 4YY

www.scouts.org.uk/join

Contents

Introduction

A code is a way of turning **information** (letters or words) into other letters or symbols.

This could be because the information needs to be kept **secret**. You encode a message to stop people reading it, and your friend can decode the message to read again. *There are lots of these codes in this book.*

Or it could be because the information is **impossible to send** without encoding it. You can't speak to a friend at the other end of a field, but you can 'talk' to him in a code like semaphore. *There are lots of these codes in this book too.*

Another reason for using a code is to give complicated information in a **quicker, simpler** way. An example would be the barcode on the back cover of this book, or a road sign (which is part of the Highway Code). *There are lots of these codes in this book as well.*

Actually, there are *loads* of codes in this book. Let's get started!

Caesar's Secrets

Julius Caesar was a Roman general two thousand years ago. He was clever and ambitious, and ended up as Emperor, in charge of the whole Roman Empire. Caesar used codes to keep secrets from his enemies.

The most well-known of Caesar's codes was simple: every letter in his message was changed to a different letter.

How to do it

1 Write out the alphabet neatly.

ABCDEFGHIJKLMNOPQRSTUVWXYZ

2 Now write the alphabet out again underneath, but start in a different place – under the J. When you reach the end of the row, go back to the beginning to finish writing letters. It should look something like this.

A B C D E F G H I J K L M
R S T U V W X Y Z A B C D

3 Here's the message you want to encode:

YOU ARE BEING WATCHED

4 Find the first letter of your message in the **top** alphabet, and write down the letter underneath it:

YOU ARE BEING WATCHED
P

What will the whole message read?

> **Your answer**
>
>
>
>
>
>
>

Answer on page 92

N O P Q R S T U V W X Y Z

E F G H I J K L M N O P Q

Now let's try decoding a Caesar code.

Here it is:

G BUPY SIO QILEYX NBCM ION

Remember you wrote the second alphabet starting from **J**? This time you will start writing at **G** – the first letter in this coded message. This first letter is called the **code key**.

1 Write out the second alphabet – make sure you start in the right place. A goes under G.

2 The code key isn't part of the coded message. This time, find the letters of the coded message in the **bottom** alphabet, and write down the letter **above** each one. So above B is **H**, then above U is **A**.

3 Can you decode the whole message?

G BUPY SIO QILEYX NBCM ION

> **Your answer**
>
>
>
>

Answer on page 92

Now try writing your own message.

See if a friend can decode it.

Wheel Out the Code Wheel

It takes a long time writing out all those alphabets for Caesar codes. You can make things easier with a **code wheel**. A code wheel is two circles of card that are fixed together in the middle so they can turn. Around the edge of each circle is an alphabet: the outer one for your plain message, and the inner one for the coded version.

How to make a code wheel

1 You need two circles of card like the ones opposite.
   a) Photocopy, scan and print or trace the page opposite.
   b) Stick the copy on to thin card (an old cereal box).
   c) Cut the circles out.

2 Make a small hole in the centre of each circle.
   a) Stick a lump of modelling clay to a table.
   b) Place the middle of one circle over the clay.
   c) Push a pencil through the card into the clay.
   d) Repeat with the other circle.

3 Fix the two circles together with a paper fastener, so they can turn.

4 Make two sets of wheels, so a friend can solve your messages as quickly as you can encode them!

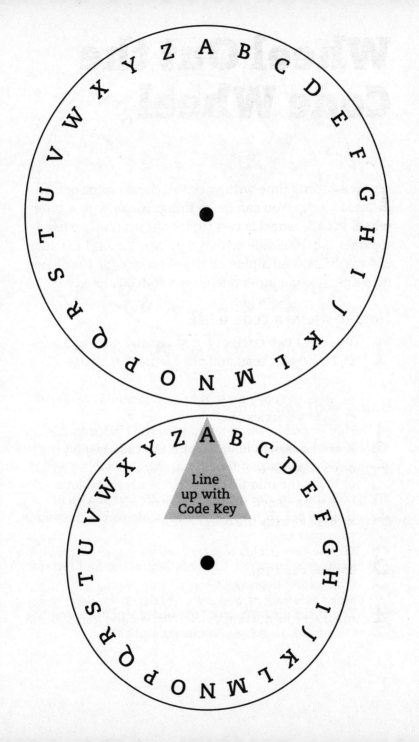

Line
up with
Code Key

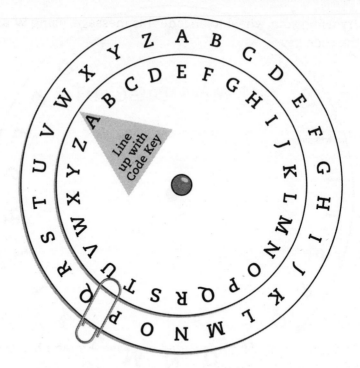

Using your code wheel

1 Pick a code key letter, and turn the circles to line up **A** on the inner alphabet with the **code key** on the outer alphabet.

2 Clip the two circles together with a paperclip or clothes peg so they don't slip while you're encoding your message.

3 Remember to write the code key as the first letter in your coded message.

4 The plain message uses the **outer** alphabet, and the coded message uses the **inner** alphabet.

Try using your wheel to encode this message, using **W** as the code key.

GET ME A BISCUIT

Your answer

And now try solving this coded message – remember, the first letter is the code key.

N TRG VG LBHEFRYS

Your answer

Answers on page 92

Now try writing your own messages and see if a friend can decode them.

If you haven't made a code wheel yet, use this one, which we've set to code key F!

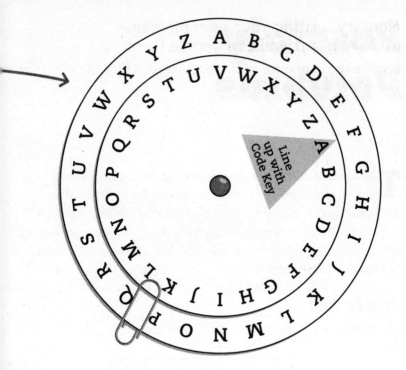

Possibly Polybius

The Caesar codes are fine, but they depend on being able to pass on the coded message. Sometimes that isn't possible. A clever Greek chap called Polybius worked out this code over two thousand years ago. It was perfect for signalling quickly to people you can see or hear – on a battlefield, for instance.

How to do it

1 Draw a five-by-five grid of squares.

2 Fill the grid with the alphabet. Yes, there isn't enough room for every letter – put I and J in the same square. As you work out the message it will become clear which of these two letters you need to use.

3 Number each row and column of the grid with numbers – along the top and down the left side, like this.

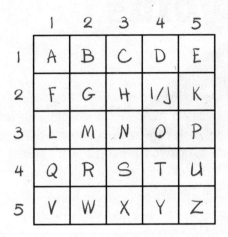

4 Every letter is in a **row** (with a number) and a **column** (with a number). So every letter can be turned into two numbers – the row first, then the column. So **H** becomes **2-3** and **E** turns into **1-5**.

5 See if you can use the grid to work out the numbers for each letter in this message:

HELP ME

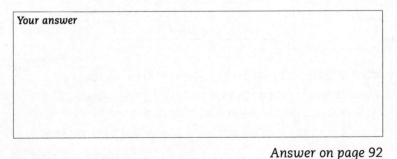

Your answer

Answer on page 92

6 There are lots of ways to send your coded message. Use a torch to **flash** it, with a little gap between numbers:

GO becomes 2-2, 3-4 – which is
flash-flash . . .
flash-flash . . .
flash-flash-flash . . .
flash-flash-flash-flash.

7 Or use a whistle or drum to send the numbers by **sound**. Write down the code for STOP so you can clap it or tap it on the table.

Your answer

Answer on page 92

Now try sending your own messages.

Write your message, then work out the code.

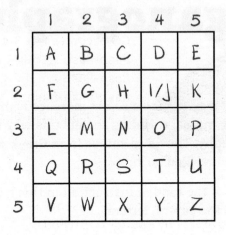

	1	2	3	4	5
1	A	B	C	D	E
2	F	G	H	I/J	K
3	L	M	N	O	P
4	Q	R	S	T	U
5	V	W	X	Y	Z

Super Steganography*

The best way to hide a secret message is in a normal-looking message. Hiding secrets this way is called **steganography**. The word comes from Greek words meaning 'concealed writing'.

Can you spot the hidden instruction in this letter? (Look at all the capital letters.)

There are lots of other ways to hide a message in a message:

- Move some letters above or below the line

- Prick a tiny hole under some letters with a pin

- Use a different colour ink or typeface for some letters (a bit obvious)

- Write a tiny message on the corner of an envelope and cover it with the stamp

Could you write your own secret this way?

* This is not a dinosaur

Greetings, friend.

Ow are you? Tom's here with me. Old Tom, you remember. He says hi. Everyone here is well. Hope you're well, I'm feeling fine. Do write back. Expect another letter soon. Or write to me instead. Unless we meet first.

Tom

Your answer

Answer on page 92

Can you find the messages in these letters?

Remember the different ways steganography can be used.

Dear Kelly,

Anna has asked again if you are coming to her party. I said I didn't know if you were allowed to, and probably wouldn't make it. Anna would really like you and Jo to come to the party if you can. George and Kitty said they are going, so do come!

Cath

Your answer

Dear Sir

Attached is the information you requested (version 2). We do not normally keep older types in stock, but we can get hold of the ones you want in a day or so. Let us know whether you need more advice.

Yours faithfully,

Greedy Gus

Your answer

Answers on page 92

Now You Don't See It, Now You Do

Another way to hide a secret in a letter is to use **invisible ink**. It's easier than you'd think to make your own!

The best way to use invisible ink is to write on an ordinary letter – on the back, or round the edges of the front. Use a cotton bud, a cocktail stick or a small brush to write with the invisible ink. Make sure it's dry before you pass on the letter.

Recipe 1

1 Mix a big spoonful of baking soda in half a glass of water. Stir it until all the powder has dissolved.

2 To reveal this ink, pour some lemon juice in a saucer and use a sponge or a piece of kitchen roll to wipe it over the back of the letter. If you haven't got lemon juice, then orange, grape or cranberry juice will do.

Recipe 2

1 Write your message with a small amount of lemon juice. If you haven't got lemon juice, then milk, apple juice or white vinegar will work.

2 To reveal these inks, you need to heat the letter carefully. Try taping it to a radiator for an hour. Or get an adult to iron it gently (put a clean sheet of paper over the letter first). It can also be warmed in a low oven (100°C) for ten minutes. **Don't use an iron or oven without asking an adult first.**

Revealing Red Cabbage

Another way to reveal messages written with either recipe is to use red cabbage water. Ask an adult to boil half a red cabbage, chopped up, in a small saucepan of water for fifteen minutes. Pour the water off into a bowl through a sieve and leave it to cool. It will be dark purple. You can save this water and use a sponge to wipe it over letters with invisible messages on.

Stick It Under the Grille

Here's a super-safe way to send a secret message to a friend: a **code grille**. This method is best for sending quite short messages.

How to do it

1 To send the message, you both need your own copy of a book – exactly the same book, obviously! It won't work if you have an old hardback version and your friend has a new paperback. You also need some tracing paper and a pencil.

2 Choose a page with lots of words on it. Place a sheet of tracing paper over the page and mark where the corners of the page are.

3 Read the page through the tracing paper until you find the first letter of your message on the page. Draw a circle round it.

4 Carry on reading, looking for the second letter, third letter, and so on. Ring each letter as you find it.

5 If you can't find the next letter you need, just draw it on the tracing paper.

6 When you've finished, write the page number in the corner of the tracing paper. Fold the tracing paper up so you can pass it to your friend secretly.

7 Your friend finds the right page in their copy of the book, puts the tracing paper on top and lines up the corners, then reads the circled letters in order.

Time for you to do some grilling!

Copy this pattern on to tracing paper, and hold it over the opposite page to reveal the hidden message.

Top right corner ↗

Nihicitiis maionsed magne sit et eossum harchil modicimus ditaque dolupta veliquiamet officaborepe aditios simolup tatquia vero di sum cus pero consend itaturepero bla qui ilibusciis pellor aspeliquam faccus autatiusa quam quas sitatem dolorio riassi totas nihil ipic tem venimporpor simpe sum et rerestiurit facero volupta quaest ommodigent et parum reicia alisit omnimus dentis et, tem quid mincima gnihit experi qui apersperro ium quis et etusamus doluptae perum nonestis ipitate vent eium andae earumquodi aut debitae nonsera vit, comnihilit, autat harum quis ulpa cupturibusa conem aut esciae nullupti non nonsend antiber umquiae natibus rerrum quaesti issimporum as molupti simus.

Ebitibus. At occus dolupicatem velic te cumque nit acerum imus, consequia cone officta tassim quo dolore velest, que dolorepta antiur, vent magnihit, aliquodi nimentore vellupt atiorerum dis qui verist que volenestia nullabo restrumet min corit, sima volorit lit alia venda. Nulluptaque nobitin tetur? Miniateni ne nusandis illupta tusdaesto offictem qui nam int dolora dolupta tiorum et am, untotas reperisciam, cum ex erorrum quatus, seque voluptatate dolorerrum hitem reius ant perum et aut labo. Molent quod maximporum, to maionse ribusci sit qui velent, seque volorum facilic iendend amustru mendandunt et pratectempor maionse. Nequunt mo dolupta exped qui cum voluptat moluptat.

Your answer

Answer on page 92

Cracking Caesar

It didn't take long for clever people to work out how to solve any Caesar code, because there are two problems with them. **Firstly**, there are only 25 different codes (you can't use A as a code key). And **secondly**, they work the same way throughout the message, swapping letters so that every A always becomes an H, for instance.

If you think a message was encoded with a Caesar code, you can just try all 25 codes (with a code wheel) to see which one works. It's even easier if you think you know a word hidden in the coded message.

For instance, if you know these messages contain the word **Caesar**, it's easy to spot which code key was used by checking the table opposite. Can you solve the messages?

1) HFJXFW MFX F GFQI MJFI

2) FYNM UFF ECFF WUYMUL

3) JURER QBRF PNRFNE YVIR

> **Your answers**
>
>
>
>

Answers on page 92

Code Key	Word
A	**CAESAR**
B	DBFTBS
C	ECGUCT
D	FDHVDU
E	GEIWEV
F	HFJXFW
G	IGKYGX
H	JHLZHY
I	KIMAIZ
J	LJNBJA
K	MKOCKB
L	NLPDLC
M	OMQEMD
N	PNRFNE
O	QOSGOF
P	RPTHPG
Q	SQUIQH
R	TRVJRI
S	USWKSJ
T	VTXLTK
U	WUYMUL
V	XVZNVM
W	YWAOWN
X	ZXBPXO
Y	AYCQYP
Z	BZDRZQ

Shop Signals

You can send a message using whatever is handy, as long as you know how the code works.

A shopkeeper sends messages across the street to her brother by arranging tins and packets in her shop window in a special way. Here's the code:

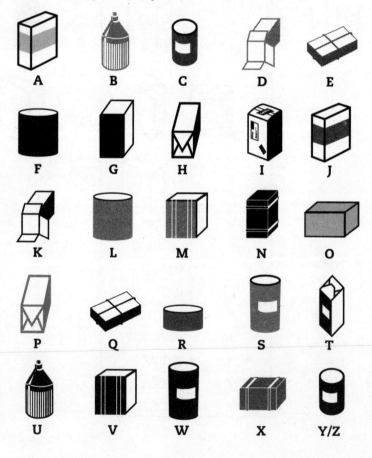

What is she saying today?

Your answer

Can you bring me
a cup of tea
please

Answer on page 93

Scrt Shrthnd

In the seventeenth century, people working on newspapers and in offices had to be able to write down speeches – which meant writing really fast! They used codes called **shorthand**.

Shorthand looks like a lot of squiggles. Each squiggle may mean more than just a letter – it could mean a sound, part of a word or all of a word. And the squiggles can be written as quickly as people talk. If no one knows how to read your shorthand, it can even make a pretty good secret code.

Famous Shorthand

Possibly the most famous shorthand user was Samuel Pepys (say it like 'peeps'). He was born in London in 1633, and lived through the English Civil War, the Fire of London and the Black Death. He also had an important job in the navy, when Britain was fighting a war with Holland. His diaries are interesting and funny, and he wrote them in shorthand – probably so he could write more quickly, but possibly so his wife couldn't read the rude bits!

How fast can you write?

Get a friend to read out the sentences below while you try to write them down at the same time.

> The quick brown fox jumps over a lazy dog. Pack my box with five dozen liquor jugs. Six zips were quickly picked from the woven jute bag. The five boxing wizards jump quickly.

Could you keep up? How many mistakes did you make? Can your friend do better than you?

And did you notice anything unusual about the sentences in the test?

Answer on page 93

Pigpen Code

The Freemasons is a secret club that's rather popular – there are millions of Masons today, divided into groups called Lodges.

In the eighteenth century, Lodge leaders sent secret messages to each other using a grid code called a pigpen. Today there are still gravestones and buildings with pigpen messages carved into them.

How to do it

1 Draw four grids and then draw in the alphabet, one letter in each space, like this. Don't forget the dots!

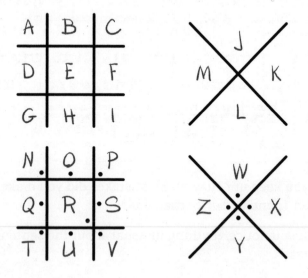

2 The code for any letter is the shape of the grid space it's in.

So A is ⌐ and O is ⌐.

Try encoding this message:

HAVE YOU SEEN MY PIG

> **Your answer**

Now try working out what this coded message says:

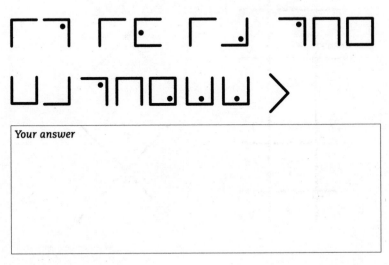

> **Your answer**

Answers on page 93

What does this message say?

Your answer

Can you encode this message?

HE IS REALLY FOWL

Your answer

Answers on page 93

Now try sending your own messages.

Write your message, then work out the code.

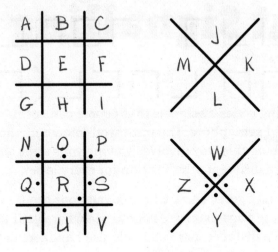

Not Waving, But Signalling

Sending codes by signals that people can see is called **semaphore**. The most well-known method of signalling this way involves waving your arms about! There is a different arm position for every letter.

These little figures show where to put your arms. Semaphore flags make it easier to see where your arms are from a distance, but you could use handkerchiefs or hats if you haven't got flags.

The pictures show what you see when you're looking at someone else's semaphore – you need to reverse arms when you're sending a semaphore message.

Key

 A (& 1)

 B (& 2)

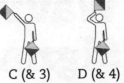 C (& 3)

 D (& 4)

 E (& 5)

 F (& 6)

 G (& 7)

 H (& 8)

 I (& 9)

 J

 K (& 0)

 L

 M

N

 O

 P

Q

R

S

T

U

 V

 W

 X

 Y

 Z

 Error or Attention

 Numbers follow

 Space or Rest

What do these messages say?

> **Your answer**

B-P's semaphore writing

Lord Baden-Powell worked out that you could write semaphore as well. Just draw the arm-shapes for each letter, joining them together into a wiggly line. Start at the top or the bottom. Adding dots between the shapes can help to make it clearer. You could then disguise the line as a pattern in the edge of a picture.

This says HELLO – can you read it?

Your answer

Answers on page 93

Try writing your name in semaphore writing.

That's Handy

You can use your hands to 'talk', using **sign language**. There are many different sign languages around the world, each with local 'accents', just like speech. Around 20,000 people use British Sign Language every day.

Soldiers also have their own simple sign language, for when they have to keep quiet on a mission.

You may have seen sign language on television, for viewers who can't hear well.

Something Special

If you've seen Something Special on CBeebies, then you've seen Justin (and Mr Tumble) using Makaton, a group of signs and pictures based on British Sign Language that even babies can learn before they speak. Here are the signs for 'mum' and 'dad'.

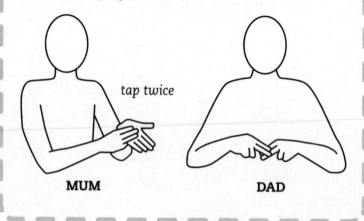

tap twice

MUM   DAD

Have a go!

You know more sign language than you think. How could you 'say' these phrases to a friend on the other side of the room, using only your hands?

Hello

Do you want a drink?

Good

Stop!

Be quiet

I can't hear you

There's a phone call for you

Come here

Go to sleep

I don't understand

Can you think of any other phrases you can 'say' with your hands?

Talking Fingers

If you think sign language is interesting, see if you and a friend can learn this version that only uses one hand.

This is the alphabet in American Sign Language. Rather than spell out whole words, you could just use the first letter – so instead of signing 'Hello James' you could sign '**H J**' instead.

What does this say?

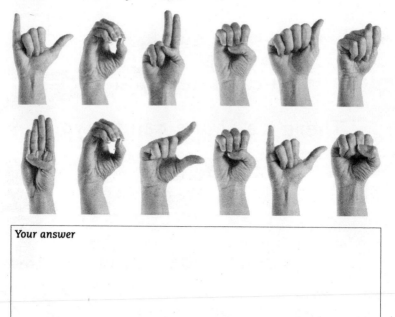

Your answer

Answer on page 93

Key

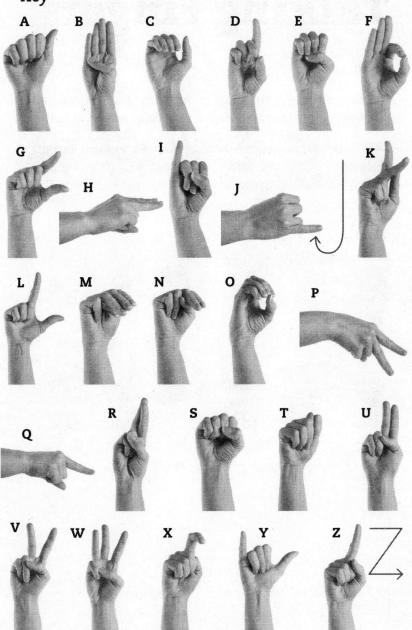

Can you read this message?

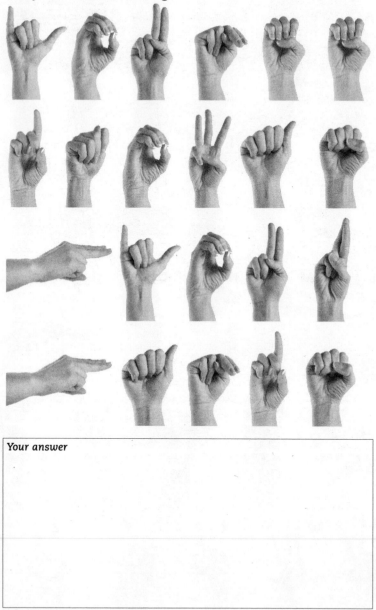

Your answer

Answer on page 93

'England Expects That Every Man Will Do His Duty'

The British navy used to use flags to send messages from ship to ship. Admiral Nelson sent this famous announcement just before the Battle of Trafalgar in 1805.

Every ship carried dozens of flags. There was a different flag for every letter of the alphabet, and every number, and others for things like asking questions. The biggest flags were almost ten metres wide!

Rather than spelling out whole words, which would take ages, Nelson used a navy code. It only used ten flags, for the numbers 0 to 9. All the words and phrases he might need were turned into numbers, using a code book. So to say 'England', which was '253', three flags were tied to a rope and hauled up the mast so that other ships could see. Then those flags were pulled down, and the flags for '269' were raised next – meaning 'expects'.

Heavy Code

The navy code books had covers made of lead. This meant they would sink quickly when they were thrown overboard, if the enemy captured your ship. It also meant they stayed still in a storm!

After signalling 'England expects that every man will do his duty', as the battle was about to begin, Nelson signalled 'Engage the enemy more closely' – which used only two number flags in code: '16'.

In just two hours the British won the battle, but Nelson was seriously wounded and died later that day.

Here are the flags for A to Z and 0 to 9. To colour them in you will need red, yellow and blue. If part of a flag has **R** in it, colour it red; if it has **Y** in it, colour it yellow; and colour a shape blue if it has a **B** in it. The other areas will be white or black.

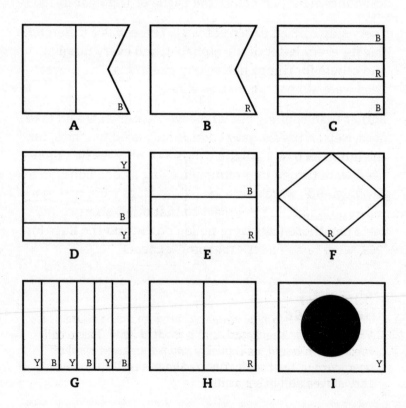

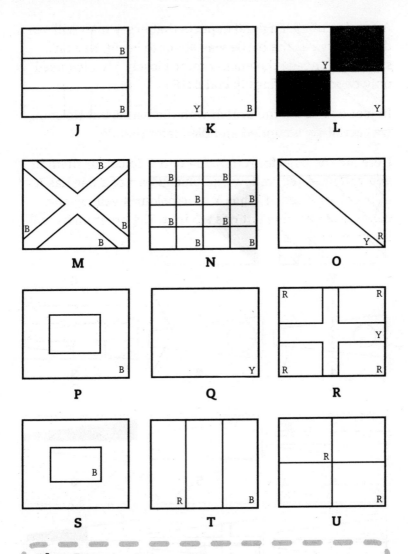

J

K

L

M

N

O

P

Q

R

S

T

U

Blue Peter

The flag for P is a blue square around a white square. It is known as the 'Blue Peter', and is hoisted by a ship to call everyone on board, as it is about to set sail and head off on a journey. That's why the TV show is called Blue Peter and has a sailing ship as its logo.

51

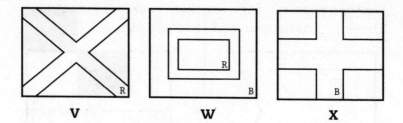

V   **W**   **X**

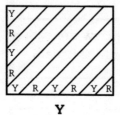 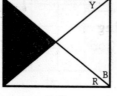

Y   **Z**   **0**

1   **2**   **3**

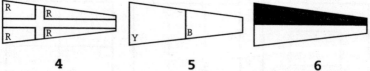

4   **5**   **6**

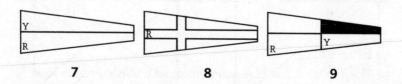

7   **8**   **9**

Now you know the flags, use them to decorate things. These flags have meanings you could use.

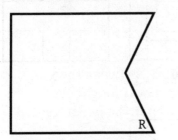

B: I am discharging dangerous cargo (for the bathroom door)

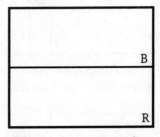

E: The crew are eating (for the kitchen)

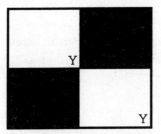

L: Infectious disease aboard, stay clear (for your bedroom door when you have a cold)

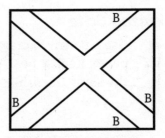

M: I have stopped moving (for when you've gone to bed)

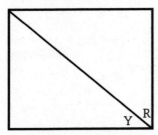

O: Man overboard (for when you've gone out)

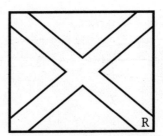

V: I require assistance (for when your homework is too hard)

Zigzag or Swap?

The American Civil War (1861–5), between the northern and southern states, was fought over slavery – the south wanted to keep it, the north wanted to ban it.

Both sides used many different codes, which often involved mixing up a message to make it unreadable. Here are two of them.

Zigzag Code

1 Use a pencil to draw a big zigzag across some lined paper. Keep it neat, so you always start and stop on the same lines, like this.

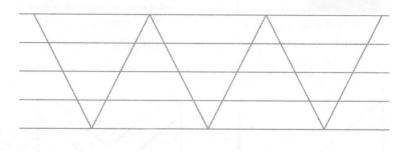

2 Write your message along the zigzag one letter at a time, with each letter going where the zigzag crosses a line. Fill the zigzag with letters if your message is too short.

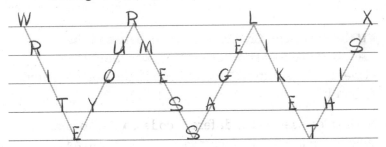

3 Copy your message out again, reading across the lines.

WRLXRUMEISIOEGKITYSAEHEST

This is what you send to your friend.

4 To unravel a zigzag message, draw another neat zigzag. This time, write the message out one line at a time, with each letter going where the line crosses the zigzag.

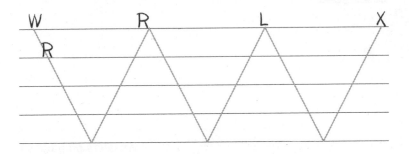

Solve these messages.

DPIXOULARDWD IFGNNNKARUAEO

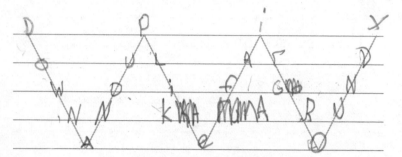

COFZATPIEKNS
IWECYUTOLIONS

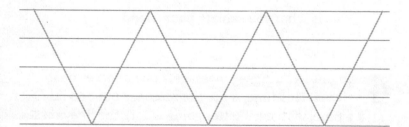

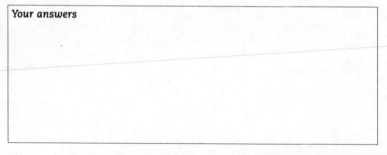

Your answers

Answers on page 93

Now try sending your own messages.

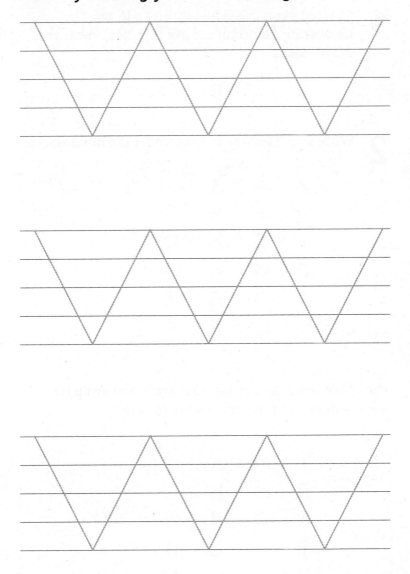

Swap Code

1 Squared paper is useful for this code. Start by numbering four columns like this. Remember the order – **2431**.

2   4   3   1

2 Write your message in rows under the numbers.

2	4	3	1
W	H	A	T
I	S	B	R
O	W	N	A
N	D	S	T
I	C	K	Y

3 Now write the message out again, but **swap** the columns so the numbers are in order.

1	2	3	4
T	W	A	H
R	I	B	S
A	O	N	W
T	N	S	D
Y	I	K	C

4 The coded message is read off **down** the columns, from left to right – ignoring the numbers.

TRATY WIONI ABNSK HSWDC

This is what you send to your friend.

5 To decode the message, write the numbers again (**2431**, remember). Then write the message down in columns, starting under the 1. Try it with this message – it's been started for you. Fill in column 2 next.

ETTSX TTHHI GOORE OTEED

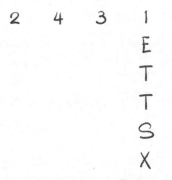

```
2   4   3   1
            E
            T
            T
            S
            X
```

6 Read the decoded message one row at a time. There may be letters at the end you can ignore – they were added to fill out the space.

Your answer

Answer on page 93

Now solve these swap codes.

COHHQ KKCOE ONWTE NKKSR

Your answer

MMOTE HAEET WYDIK ONNSA

Your answer

Answers on page 93

Baden-Powell's Butterflies

B-P worked for British military intelligence in the late nineteenth century. He travelled around the Mediterranean, pretending to be a butterfly collector while secretly drawing military forts, noting the position and size of their guns.

Here is one of the forts that Baden-Powell spied on. He noted the position and size of the guns.

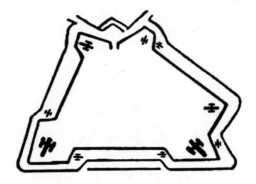

Then he hid the plan in a drawing of a butterfly. Some of the blobs on the wings show the size of the guns, and lines lead from the blobs to their position in the fort.

Here are some other drawings that need disguising. What can you turn them into so your enemies won't suspect you are spying?

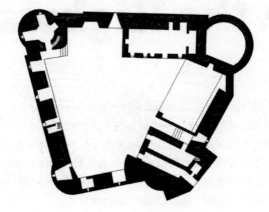

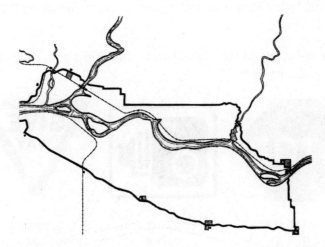

My Way on the Highway

In the 1950s, British road signs were very confusing. When drivers went faster, they didn't have time to read complicated signs as they drove past them. To make things worse, different places had different styles of sign. To end the confusion, the Highway Code was introduced: a standard set of bright, clear signs.

All round signs give **orders** – things you have to do. All triangular signs give **warnings** – things you should look out for. And other shapes give different instructions. The signs we have today were designed and drawn by just two people, Jock Kinneir and Margaret Calvert, between 1957 and 1967.

Here are a few of the signs you should help your parents to watch out for!

Stop at the white line ahead

Speed cameras ahead

Give way to traffic at junction

20mph speed limit · No entry · No stopping

No cycling · No right turn · All traffic must go this way

Wild animals · Slippery road · Children

Pedestrians on road · Roadworks · Railway crossing with no barrier

Can You Get There from Here?

Make your way across town from the start to the finish, obeying all the traffic signs on the way.

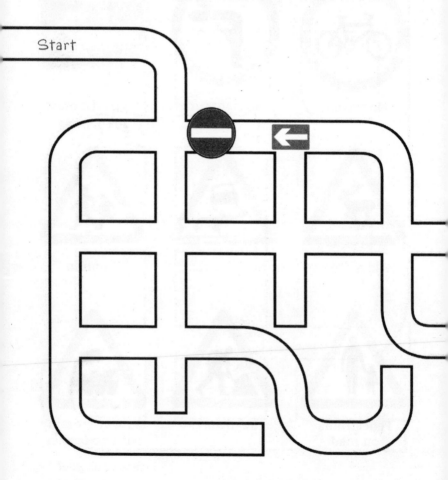

Start

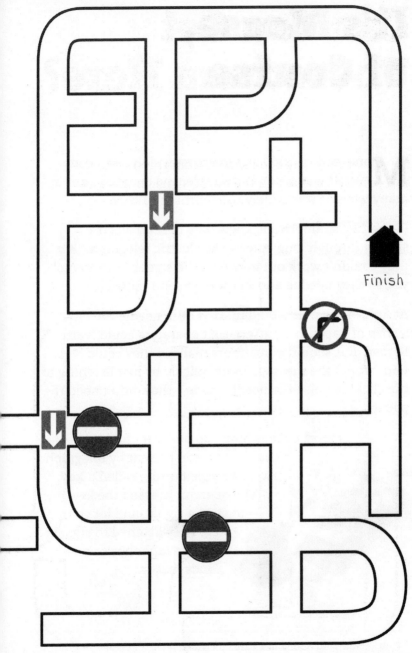

Finish

Answer on page 94

It's Morse, of Course

Morse code is probably the most widely used code ever. It was quick and simple, and could be sent in many ways. It was widely used until the 1990s.

In the 1840s, Americans knew how to send electric signals through long wires – the electric telegraph.* But they couldn't work out how turn the signals into sound yet, so they needed another way to send messages.

At first the signals would make a little needle tap on to a strip of paper in a pattern that operators could learn to read. But soon the operators realized they could understand the message more quickly by just listening to the clicking noise the needle made – they didn't need the paper.

Morse code is made up of short and long signals that could be sent by telegraph with a single button, called a **key**. The operator pressed the key to start a signal, and let go to stop. They listened to signals with headphones or a loudspeaker.

---

* Poles holding up phone lines are still called telegraph poles.

Operators learned and practised Morse by saying the codes, 'dit' or 'di' for a short signal and 'dah' for a long signal. So **A** is 'di-dah'. The international distress signal, **SOS**, is 'di-di-dit dah-dah-dah di-di-dit'.

Morse worked well by telegraph, between two places linked by a wire. It worked even better by radio, as it meant messages could finally be sent to ships at sea, or aeroplanes, or armies on the move. It still worked when the radio signal was too weak to transmit voices.

Morse can be sent quickly by expert operators, because letters that are more common in English, like E and T, are shorter and easier to send than uncommon letters like X and Q.

Key

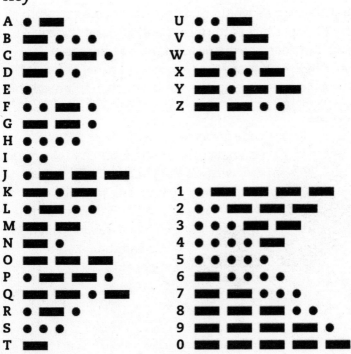

Murderer caught by Morse

In 1910 Henry Crippen killed his wife and tried to escape to Canada by ship with his girlfriend Ethel. The captain was suspicious, because Ethel was disguised as a boy. He sent a Morse message back to the police in Britain, and a detective set off after the couple on a faster ship. He arrested Crippen before he landed in Canada.

What does this Morse message say?

−.−./−−−/−−/.

−−.−/..−/../−.−./−.−/.−../−.−−

−/./.−   ../...

.−./././.−/−../−.−−

Your answer

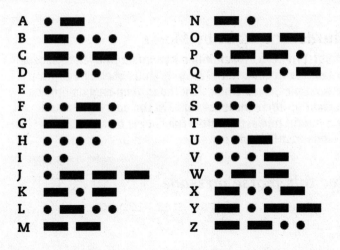

Can you write the Morse for this message?

Will there be chips

Your answer

Answers on page 94

Flash Bang Morse

Morse can be sent in many ways apart from the telegraph or radio. You could flash a light; ships used to do this to send messages when they thought enemies might be picking up their radio signals. Or you can tap the code out on a metal pipe – prisoners have done this to 'talk' to their friends in other cells.

Solve this morse message.

-·/---/- ·-/-·/-·--

--/---/·-·/· -/····/·

-··/---/--· ·-/-/·

-·--/---/··-/·-·/···

Your answer

Answer on page 94

Your Very Own Code Book

Telegraph wires connected the whole world by 1900. But the public didn't have to learn Morse code to use them – they just went to the Telegraph Office. You wrote out your message on a form, and an operator sent it by Morse code. At the other end your message was typed out on paper and delivered straight away by a messenger. This was called a **telegram**.

You paid for every word you wrote, so telegrams were short, used codes, and missed words out. Sounds familiar? Yes, they were tweeting and texting over a hundred years ago!

To save money on telegrams you could buy a code book that turned long common phrases into single words. There were several different ones, often written to help businesses dealing with suppliers and agents in other countries – sending telegrams abroad was REALLY expensive!

'Happy Birthday to You'

You could pay a bit extra to have a pretty printed telegram for a special occasion, like a birthday. Or you could pay more and have your message sung by the messenger – a Singing Telegram. You can still get Singing Telegrams today, usually involving fancy dress!

For example, the *Unicode Universal Telegraphic Phrase-Book* said that instead of sending 'I am unable to work today, send a messenger with any letters' you should just send **Anxietas**. **Memoratus** meant 'Have not received any letter from you. Write at once.' **Abneptis** meant 'Had an accident, come as quickly as you can.'

Your Code Words

You could use a similar system to send messages quickly and secretly. You need to agree with your friends what these words mean to **you** – here are some suggestions to get you started. Write out a copy of your code book for your friend and *keep it secret*!

I can't talk now, people are listening	**Aurifex**
Meet me at our usual place	**Absolvo**
I can't meet as we arranged	**Agilitas**
. . . .	**Candesco**
. . . .	**Chelonia**
. . . .	**Curiosus**
. . . .	**Deformis**
. . . .	**Dormisco**
. . . .	**Folium**

.... **Forfex**

.... **Imprecor**

.... **Inflammo**

.... **Majestas**

.... **Mordax**

.... **Nimio**

.... **Nugator**

.... **Oblivio**

.... **Opulus**

.... **Parumper**

.... **Propola**

.... **Rejectus**

.... **Rigatio**

.... **Saxifer**

.... **Sigma**

.... **Venetus**

.... **Viridis**

Bravo, Charlie!

Radio messages weren't always clear and easy to hear. The problems got even worse when people from different countries were trying to speak to each other. Spelling out words could be confusing, because some letters sound alike – was that M or N?

The answer was to use a word instead of each letter of the alphabet. This is called a **phonetic alphabet**. There have been different versions over the years. In the First World War this was used:

Ack	Beer	Charlie	Don	Edward
Freddie	Gee	Harry	Ink	Johnnie
King	London	eMma	Nuts	Oranges
Pip	Queen	Robert	eSses	Toc
Uncle	Vic	William	X-ray	Yorker
Zebra				

In the Second World War, soldiers were using this version:

Able	Baker	Charlie	Dog	Easy
Fox	George	How	Item	Jig
King	Love	Mike	Nan	Oboe
Peter	Queen	Roger	Sugar	Tare
Uncle	Victor	William	X-ray	Yoke
Zebra				

In the 1950s, a standard phonetic alphabet was chosen for all international radio signals. Ships, aircraft, armies and the police all over the world use it today.

Alpha	**Bravo**	**Charlie**
Delta	**Echo**	**Foxtrot**
Golf	**Hotel**	**India**
Juliet	**Kilo**	**Lima**
Mike	**November**	**Oscar**
Papa	**Quebec**	**Romeo**
Sierra	**Tango**	**Uniform**
Victor	**Whiskey**	**X-ray**
Yankee	**Zulu**	

How many of these words do you know?
Can you write your name with them below?

Have a go!

Wartime Tweets

You may feel very modern putting LOL at the end of your texts. But soldiers writing home in the early twentieth century did exactly the same thing.

They were only given small cards to write on, to save paper and postal costs. This meant there was only room for a few words, so they used **acronyms**, words where every letter stands for another word – like LOL stands for Laugh Out Loud.

What do you think these acronyms meant when soldiers wrote them ninety years ago?

SWALK

a) Sealed With A Loving Kiss

b) Shall We Always Love Kindly

ITALY

a) I Try And Like You

b) I Trust And Love You

HOLLAND

a) Hope Our Love Lasts And Never Dies

b) Have One Last Look At New Deal

WALES

a) With A Love Eternal, Sweetheart

b) We Are Laughing Every Second

FRANCE

a) Final Romantic Advice: Never Chew Eggs

b) Friendship Remains And Never Can End

BOLTOP

a) Better On Lips Than On Paper

b) Boring Old Lady Trying On Pants

Answers on page 94

Crossword Code

Secret messages to spies have been hidden in newspapers – in the **crossword**. Solve this crossword, and then read the letters in the grey squares to spell out a message. All the answers are in this book.

Across

1   What was the Freemasons' code called?

3   Who commanded the British Navy at Trafalgar?

6   What sign language is used on *Something Special*?

9   What is a message sent by waving flags called?

10   What is a message sent by electric telegraph called?

11   Who was the Roman general who became emperor?

Down

2   What is the phonetic alphabet word for E?

4   What method helped Samuel Pepys to write quickly?

5   What vegetable can reveal invisible messages?

6   Which code is made of dits and dahs?

7   Which London airport has the code LHR?

8   Which Greek invented a code better than Caesar's?

Answers on page 95

Read Your Cornflakes

You must have seen these little pictures on
packaging – but do you what do they mean?
Can you match each symbol to its meaning?

Fragile

Keep dry

This way up

Can be recycled

Dispose of this
packaging carefully

Made from responsibly managed
wood

The person who supplied this
product was paid a fair price

This product meets European
safety standards

Answers on page 95

Calling Inspector Sands

Some places use special codes to tell staff something without the public knowing. These are all phrases you might hear in a rail station, shopping centre or hospital. Four are ordinary messages that the public can understand, and four are codes for the staff that have a secret meaning. Can you spot the important announcements?

The store will be closing in ten minutes.

Code Adam, Code Adam.

Code Blue, room 417.

Passengers are reminded to take all their luggage with them.

Who is Mr Sands?

Old theatres were dangerous places, because they had lots of candles and gaslights that could catch fire. So buckets of sand were kept handy, to throw over fires and put them out. And if anyone spotted a fire, they would shout 'Mr Sands!' rather than 'fire!' – which might make people in the audience panic.

Calling Inspector Sands, Inspector Sands to Platform 6.

Cleaner to the checkouts, please.

Mister Strong to the main entrance, please.

Could Mr Roberts come to reception where his daughter is waiting for him.

Answers on page 96

Where in the World?

LHR = London Heathrow

BOS = Boston

LAX = Los Angeles

MEX = Mexico City

MAD = Madrid

Every **airport** in the world has its own three-letter code. When you check in your luggage to go on holiday, the code for your destination is put on your bags so they get sent to the right place.

This map shows the location of ten airports and their codes. Can you connect the names to the right places?

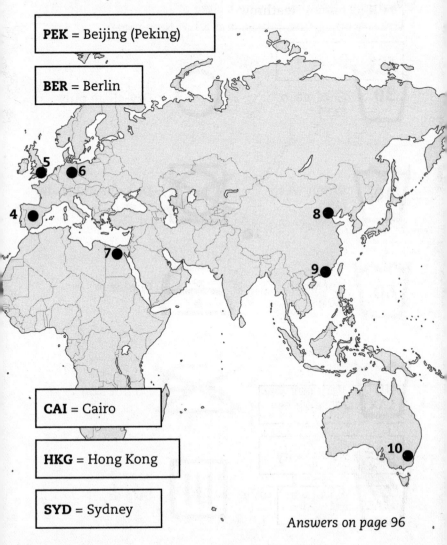

PEK = Beijing (Peking)

BER = Berlin

CAI = Cairo

HKG = Hong Kong

SYD = Sydney

Answers on page 96

Sorted

Clothes have codes on their labels that explain how they should be washed. Here are some of the pictures you see on clothes labels, and what they mean.

30° Cool wash (30°)

Dry-clean only

40° Warm wash (40°)

Do not tumble-dry

60° Hot wash (60°)

Cool iron

90° Very hot wash (90°)

Do not iron

Hand wash only

Drip dry

Can you sort these items into the right baskets?

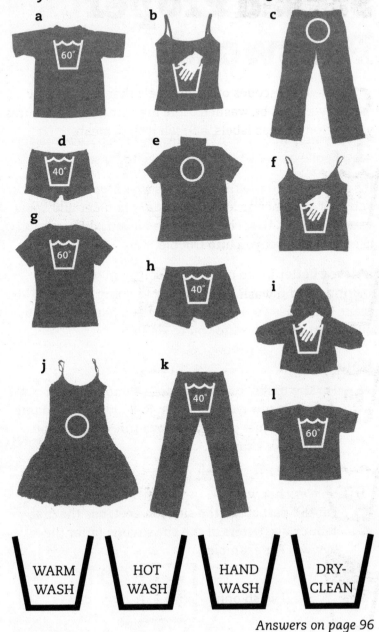

Answers on page 96

Pick a Proper Password

They may not seem like codes, but the passwords you choose when you're online need to be secret.

It's a bad idea to use the same password for every website you visit. If someone looks over your shoulder and spots your password, they could get into all your different accounts and get you into trouble.

It's even better if you can remember them without writing them down. There's a trick to doing this – you make your passwords from two parts: a part about you, and a part about the site you're visiting.

How to do it

1 For the part about you, choose something you can definitely always remember. It could be your name (all of it or just part), your favourite colour or an animal. For example:

CHRIS   RED   FISH

2 For the part about the site you visit, use the first four or five letters of the site's name (after the 'www'). For example:

FACE   MATH   YOUT

3 The whole password is both parts together. For example:

CHRISFACE

CHRISMATH

CHRISYOUT

4 To make it harder to guess, mix up capital and small letters in the password.

CHRISface

chrisMATH

cHrIsYoUt

5 And if you want to make your passwords really really good, swap some letters with numbers or other characters. These are good swaps, because the numbers look a bit like the letters and are easy to remember:

1 for I or i   **2** for Z or z   **3** for E or e

4 for A or a   **5** for S or s   **6** for G or g

7 for L or l   **8** for B or b   **0** for O or o

So now your passwords look like these:

CHRI5f4c3

chrI5M4TH

cHrI5YoUt

No one will **ever** guess those!

Answers

Caesar's Secrets

Page 7: PFL RIV SVZEX NRKTYVU

Page 8: HAVE YOU WORKED THIS OUT

Wheel Out the Code Wheel

Page 13: W KIX QI E FMWGYMX
GET IT YOURSELF

Possibly Polybius

Page 17: 2-3/1-5/3-1/3-5 3-2/1-5

Page 18: 4-3/4-4/3-4/3-5

Super Steganography

Page 21: GO TO THE HIDEOUT

Page 22: Read the letters with dots under them.
I DON'T WANT TO GO EITHER!

Page 23: Read the letters moved up or down.
HAVE YOU GOT ANY SWEETS

Stick It Under the Grille

Page 29: MEET ME AFTER SCHOOL IN THE TREE HOUSE
BRING SOME FOOD

Cracking Caesar

Page 30: 1) CAESAR HAS A BALD HEAD, code key F.
2) LET'S ALL KILL CAESAR, code key U.
3) WHERE DOES CAESAR LIVE, code key N.

Shop Signals
Page 33: CAN YOU BRING ME A CUP OF TEA PLEASE

Scrt Shrthnd
Page 35: All the sentences in the writing test contain every single letter of the alphabet. Sentences like this are called **pangrams.**

Pigpen Code
Page 37:

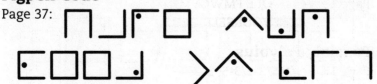

IT IS IN THE BATHROOM

Page 38: DON'T TRUST THE CHICKEN

Not Waving, But Signalling
Page 42: HAPPY BIRTHDAY

Page 43: THANKS VERY MUCH

Talking Fingers
Page 46: YOU EAT BOGEYS

Page 48: YOU NEED TO WASH YOUR HANDS

Zigzag or Swap?
Page 56: DOWN AND UP LIKE A FAIRGROUND
CAN YOU STOP IT NOW I FEEL SICK

Page 59: TO GET TO THE OTHER SIDE

Page 60: KNOCK KNOCK WHO'S THERE
HOW MANY MEN DOES IT TAKE

Can You Get There from Here?
Page 66:

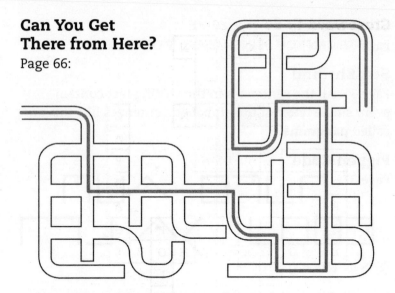

It's Morse, of Course
Page 70: COME QUICKLY TEA IS READY
Page 71: • – – / • • / • – • • / • – • •
– / • • • • / • / • – • / •
– • • • / •
– • – • / • • • • / • • / • – – • / • • •
Page 72: NOT ANY MORE THE DOG ATE YOURS

Wartime Tweets
Page 78–9:
SWALK = Sealed With A Loving Kiss
ITALY = I Trust And Love You
HOLLAND = Hope Our Love Lasts And Never Dies
WALES = With A Love Eternal, Sweetheart
FRANCE = Friendship Remains And Never Can End
BOLTOP = Better On Lips Than On Paper

Crossword Code Page 80–81:

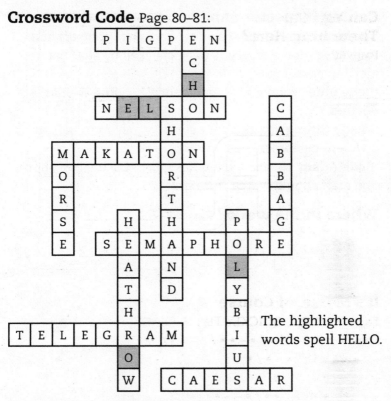

The highlighted words spell HELLO.

Read Your Cornflakes Page 82–3:

Can be recycled		®	The person who supplied this product was paid a fair price
Keep dry		CE	This product meets European safety standards
This way up		FSC ®	Made from responsibly managed wood
Fragile			Dispose of this packaging carefully

Calling Inspector Sands Page 84–5:

'Inspector Sands' means a fire alarm has gone off in a railway station and needs to be checked by staff before alerting passengers.

'Code Blue' is a medical emergency, needing special doctors.

'Mister Strong' is asking for security guards to help with a violent customer.

'Code Adam' means a child has gone missing in a shop and staff should watch the exits.

Where in the world? Page 86–7:

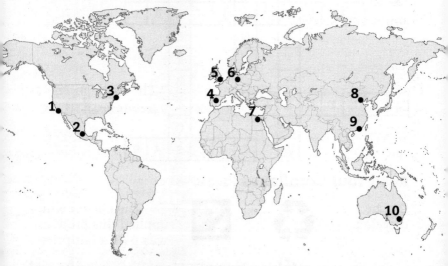

1 = LAX/Los Angeles, 2 = MEX/Mexico City, 3 = BOS/Boston,
4 = MAD/Madrid, 5 = LHR/London Heathrow,
6 = BER/Berlin, 7 = CAI/Cairo, 8 = PEK/Beijing,
9 = HKG/Hong Kong, 10 = SYD/Sydney.

Sorted Page 89:

Warm wash: d, h and k. Hot wash: a, g and l.
Hand wash: b, f and i. Dry-clean: c, e and j.